Go Right
short stories

Sara Roberts Jones

Acknowledgments

Many thanks to my mom and the rest of my family—they always read my stuff and laugh at my jokes. Thanks especially to my sister Lauren, who read early versions of these stories and said they were good. I think she was just being nice, but it gave me the encouragement I needed to actually *make* them good.

Thanks also to Synonymous, for our monthly dose of creativity and coffee; the Writerlies, for our quarterly dose of writing and hard root beer; my online friends who get pulled into brainstorming sessions and who check my details for accuracy; Deidre, for her unflagging enthusiasm and help; and Lee Ann at Illuminations Editing. Many others deserve thanks as well, because they also read my stuff and laugh at my jokes.

I'm very grateful to my kids, who think I'm kind of cool for writing books.

And deepest gratitude to Darren, who has done all he possibly can to help me reach my dreams—including giving me directions that do not include words like "north" or "right."

Thank you.

Contents

Intersections

A high wind blew through Gilly Valley overnight, pushing an old tree across the intersection of West Parkins Boulevard and Ollie Pope Road. The road crew took care of the tree and moved on. They didn't notice that they'd knocked the road sign askew.

The next day, McKee Langley took the wrong road.

The Langleys were heading to a birthday weekend for an old friend; they had fifty miles to go, and not quite enough time to get there. They'd left the highway for the haphazard roads of Gilly Valley—a town they didn't know, and didn't particularly want to.

Cheryl was reading handwritten directions off a piece of notebook paper. She glanced up in time to see the off-kilter street sign.

"Go right!" she exclaimed. "That's our turn!"

McKee hit the Durango's brakes and veered onto the side road. Behind them, an irate blue minivan honked as it flew past.

"McKee! I didn't say get us killed!"

"You told me to go right," McKee said. "I went right."

"Would you please stop it?"

"Stop what?"

"Sulking. You've been sulking ever since we left home."

"I'm not sulking. I'm confused. I don't see why Kathy can't bring her own darn china to her own darn niece instead of getting us to do it."

"I *offered*," Cheryl reminded him. "I was being *neighborly*. It's not very far out of our way and Kathy can't really spare two hours one-way just to deliver a couple of boxes."

"Maybe she can fill in for me at practice then. How's she with the fiddle? Three-stringed fiddle if one breaks."

"It's not my fault you forgot your extra strings."

"Didn't say it was."

"See, this is why I didn't tell you about the china until this morning. Gave you less time to stew about it."

"I thought I was sulking. Now I stew?"

"Yes. You stew and you sulk and you take forever to come to a decision."

"Good thing I've got people to rush me into them."

"I'm not people. I'm your wife."

The joke was a staple of their twenty-six years of marriage. Cheryl said it as a peace offering. McKee twitched his mouth in acknowledgement and turned on the CD player.

They'd listened to the song five times already, but Cheryl was used to that. The Dusty Road bluegrass band was building its repertoire, and it was McKee who chose and adapted most of the music. She put in earbuds and started her own music on her phone.

Then McKee jabbed the power button and the music stopped. "I don't think we came the right way."

Cheryl pulled out her earbuds. "Yes, we did." She pointed to the paper on her knee. "We're on West Parkins Boulevard. In about half a mile, there should be a turn—Spitup Bottom."

"What?"

"Well, that's what it looks like. Kathy's handwriting is atrocious."

"So are her directions. There's no turn as far as I can see."

Cheryl looked up, mouth open to object. The long, flat expanse of road stretched in front of her, unbroken pasture on either side.

McKee added, "I think we should have taken the road on the left back there."

"The sign said this is West Parkins! Let's drive a little more and see if we find Spitup."

McKee raised his eyebrows. "I can arrange some spit-up, if that's what you really want." He swerved the Durango drunkenly on the deserted highway. "You've got strange hobbies, woman."

"You should see the kind of people I marry," Cheryl replied.

"I'm not people . . ." McKee didn't bother to finish, having scored his point.

He turned his music back on, and Cheryl gazed ahead expectantly to alert him to Spitup Bottom. After three miles, they saw a road marker, but it was for a private drive called Angelina Avenue. The road continued past old houses, a mechanic's shop in an actual garage, and a sign for a highway they didn't want to take.

Finally Cheryl admitted defeat. "All right, we'll go back and take that left fork."

But McKee didn't slow down. "I see a gas station. We need to fill up anyway, and we can ask about those directions."

The station was a small, greasy building with a lettered sign: "Ev rett Qwik Stop Co d Drinks. Fresh Ba t." McKee pulled the silver Durango up to the pump. He headed into the station with the directions in his hand. Cheryl, getting out to fill the tank, called, "Get me some water, hon."

The older man behind the counter glanced up as McKee approached with two bottles of water from the cooler. McKee pushed the directions toward him. "I think we got turned around. Can you help us find . . . Spigot Bottom?" He thought spigot sounded better, although Cheryl was right; it did look like Kathy had written *Spitup*.

"You mean Spillout Bottom," answered the man, whom McKee assumed to be "Ev rett." "You're a-ways out of your way. Take this road back till you get to an intersection . . ."

"Got it," McKee replied. "Thanks."

"No problem."

Cheryl stuck her head in the door. "McKee, could you grab me some chips, too?"

McKee added a bag of sour cream and onion chips to their purchases, thanked Everett again, and returned to the truck.

*

As the door closed behind McKee, Everett's phone rang. He picked it up with a leisurely, "Qwick Stop."

"Dad?" said a calm but anxious voice on the other end. "I think I need to get to the hospital. I called Justin, but there's no way he can be here in under an hour. Can you drive me?"

Everett was already switching off his *Open* sign. "I'll be there in fifteen minutes, sweetie. Just hang on."

He shut down the store, locked the door, and started up his battered blue Chevy truck. Hazard lights flashing, he accelerated as quickly as the old truck would allow down Ollie Pope Road.

The only vehicle he passed was the Durango, which pulled over to let him by.

He whipped onto Angelina Avenue and pulled up at the small brick house even sooner than he'd promised.

*

The dust was still settling when McKee pulled back onto the road. He and Cheryl were both disconcerted by the sudden appearance and disappearance of the blue truck. "Hope everything's all right," said Cheryl.

"Everybody's in a hurry," McKee grumbled, and turned up his music.

They returned to the fork in the road and took what appeared to be the wrong turn, but evidently wasn't. Half a mile down West Parkins Boulevard, they found Spillout Bottom.

"That name's not much of an improvement, if you ask me," said Cheryl.

Spillout Bottom was a two-lane highway infested with shopping centers and red lights. McKee switched off his music and crept along with traffic, his shoulders tense. Cheryl watched the side roads. "We're looking for West North Street . . . who named these streets? There it is. See the Taco Bell? It's a right turn there."

"So I should go left?"

"Please don't. We might get stuck in this town forever."

McKee turned off Spillout onto a quiet residential street. Cheryl directed him to a split-level house that looked just like the houses on either side of it. He stopped in the driveway and said, "I don't think anybody's home."

"How can you tell? The garage is closed."

He pointed to the green and red plastic box overflowing with toys on the porch. "They've got kids. Kids have stuff. No way do they have room to park in the garage."

"Your band takes up our garage."

"See? Nobody parks in a garage. Just leave the china on the porch with a note."

Cheryl hesitated. McKee looked at her out of the corner of his eye and added, "And I bet we'd have time to stop at that Taco Bell for a burrito."

Cheryl laughed. "Okay, you win. Help me carry the boxes."

While McKee carefully stacked the boxes of china next to the toy box, Cheryl wrote a note on the back of Kathy's directions. Before they could finish, a minivan pulled into the driveway.

"They're not parking in the garage," McKee pointed out.

"They probably think we're breaking in and don't want to get close to us!" Cheryl hurried out to the van.

The driver rolled down her window and listened to Cheryl's rushed explanation. She nodded. The side doors opened and three kids spilled out. One of them carried a guitar case.

McKee strolled up as Cheryl was saying goodbye. "I see your son plays guitar. Any place around here to get new strings for a fiddle?"

Kathy's niece looked thoughtful. "We get ours at the music store on Spillout. I think they've got violin strings." She dug in her purse and found a wrinkled business card. "Here you go. But they close at five, so you'll have to hurry."

"Naturally," McKee grumbled.

"You owe me a burrito," Cheryl reminded him as they got into their truck.

"That was just a bribe to get us out of here quick. And she showed up after all."

"Not my fault. Pay up, buddy."

McKee was relieved to find that there was an entrance to Taco Bell at the end of West North Street. As he paid for the food at the drive-through window, Cheryl glanced at the line of traffic inching past on Spillout Bottom. "Hey, look. There's that old truck again."

The old blue Chevy was driving too close to the car in front of it. "He's still got the hazards on," McKee said. The light changed to red, but the truck pushed through the intersection anyway.

"Wonder if he's heading for a hospital," Cheryl said. "Hope it's not far from here."

"Me too," said McKee. "Because nobody's going anywhere very fast."

Cheryl shot him a look. "Should suit you just fine."

"Nope, it doesn't," McKee replied, his mouth full of nachos. "I'd rather be in my garage tuning up."

They edged into traffic. An incremental mile later, Cheryl ventured to ask, "Do we really have to stop and get new strings right now?"

"I need extras on hand. What if one breaks?"

"But we might make it to Nancy's birthday on time if we just keep going."

"No we won't." McKee spotted the music store. He cut across traffic, incurring the wrath of a shiny Subaru, and sailed into the parking lot. He pulled up to the glass-front shop at ten minutes till five.

When he returned he returned, he looked more cheerful. "Got them! Not the best quality, but they'll work. I'd never have seen this place from the road." He helped himself to another of Cheryl's nachos.

"Good thing we stopped to talk to Kathy's niece," Cheryl said smugly.

McKee ignored this. "And the guy in there says that if we take the street two lights up, we can get back to the highway and bypass the rest of this mess."

"Thank goodness," Cheryl sighed.

It was several minutes before McKee managed to turn onto Spillout Bottom. They moved forward with the traffic in unsettling little lurches. McKee turned on his music, then turned it back off.

Cheryl looked at the clock. "We're hopelessly late."

"Not my fault," McKee said tightly.

"I didn't say it was. Is that our road?" She pointed to an intersection about five hundred feet ahead. "Charmingdale Avenue? These road names!" She paused. "That jeep wants in. Good luck, buddy."

A dusty yellow Jeep waited on Charmingdale Avenue, nosing over the line, trying to make a left. With no turn arrow, his prospects were bleak. Four vehicles back, McKee took pity. When he reached the intersection, he stopped and waved. The Jeep accelerated quickly into the opening as the light turned red.

Cheryl risked a complaint. "McKee!"

McKee finally gave in to his temper. "It was one car! Let's say it's *his* fault we're late. It's sure not the person who *insisted* that we run a stupid errand—"

"Right, and I just had to get new strings here that I couldn't possibly get anywhere else!"

"If some people hadn't rushed me this morning, I wouldn't have left mine on the table!"

"*I'm not people!*" Cheryl shouted.

McKee hunched his shoulders and fumed. As soon as the light turned green, he whipped onto Charmingdale. Cheryl gripped her seat but didn't speak.

On Charmingdale Avenue, the traffic thinned out. They spotted a black and white sign directing them to the interstate.

McKee relaxed. He broke the silence with, "Let's say it's Kathy's fault we're late."

"Sounds good," Cheryl said. "And we're not coming back home this way."

"Absolutely not," McKee said firmly. "I'm beyond done with this place."

He picked up speed. The silver Durango disappeared down the highway.

*

Justin Richmond parked his dusty yellow Jeep at the hospital and catapulted out of the driver's seat. He ran through the revolving doors to the information desk. "Angelina Richmond?" he said breathlessly.

"Room 304," answered the nurse.

Justin took the stairs two at a time, and didn't bother to knock as he burst into the delivery room. Angelina was sitting on the wide white hospital bed, an IV taped to her arm. She wore the gown she'd bought for the occasion, white with blue bunnies on it. Everett sat on the beige vinyl couch, looking uneasy.

"How are you doing, Angie?" Justin asked urgently.

Angelina smiled, then grimaced as a contraction set in. She reached for his hand and he squeezed hers encouragingly. After a minute, she relaxed and smiled again.

Everett got to his feet. "I'll be getting on back to the store. Call me when!"

"We will. Thank you so much, Dad," said Angelina.

Everett slipped out, happy to return to his Qwick Stop on Ollie Pope Road.

"I'm doing fine," Angelina said, a little short of breath. "The doctor says I still have a while to go. I'm so glad you made it!"

"Yeah—I would have been later but some people let me in on Spillout."

"God bless people! Hey, Dad came across an interesting name today. What do you think of McKee?"

Justin raised his eyebrows. "That's kind of weird."

"That's what you say about all the names I like. We're going to have to name this little boy something."

"I told you, I like Track. Short for Tractor."

"Justin!"

Another contraction set in. Justin cringed as he watched her endure it. As it subsided, he adjusted her gown around her knees. "McKee, huh? Well, Mack's a lot like Track. I can do that."

"Great." Angelina took a deep breath and patted her belly. "Okay, McKee, time to go. Hurry up."

The end

Jimmy's Pizza Pie

21

June 12, 1955
From: Alice
To: Helen

Dear (daughter!) Helen,

Well, you're officially Mrs. James Burke! Glad to hear that you and Jimmy had a nice wedding trip (I guess I have to stop calling him Jimmy now). Your yellow kitchen and green curtains sound very cheery. I don't know whether robin's-egg blue or turquoise would look nicer for your living room. Let me know what you decide.

I'm enclosing one of Jimmy's (oops) favorite recipes. He came home from college his first year talking about pizza pies so I found this recipe in a magazine and started making it for him. He loves it. I forgot to include it when I sent his last box, so here it is in its own letter.

Lots of love from your "other mother,"

Alice

Jimmy's Pizza Pie *(from a Norbert Mustard advertisement in House&Home magazine)*

For the Pizza Crust
2 Cups Biscuit Mix
2 tbsps Norbert's Fine Yellow Mustard
1/2 Cups Milk

    Measure mix into a bowl. Stir mustard into milk; blend into mix. Knead 1 minute on board dusted with biscuit mix. Roll to fit a 12-in. pizza pan. Prick surface with fork. Bake in hot oven (425) 5–7 minutes or until set; remove from oven. Reduce heat to moderate (375).

For the Pizza Filling
2 Cans (8-oz) tomato sauce
1 tbsp sugar
1 tbsp minced onion
2 tbsps Norbert's Fine Yellow Mustard
1/4 tsp oregano

1 lb bulk pork sausage, cooked and drained
1 Cup Cheddar cheese
2 tbsps grated Parmesan cheese

    Combine tomato sauce, sugar, onion, mustard, and oregano; bring to a boil; simmer 10 min. Pour into partially baked crust. Sprinkle with half of

Cheddar, then sausage, then remaining Cheddar, top with Parmesan. Return to oven; bake 12–15 min or until cheese melts and crust is deep golden brown. Yield: 6 servings.

September 27, 1966
From: Helen
To: Janie

Dear Janie,

Here's the recipe you asked for. Your mother sent it to me right after Jim and I got married. I had to write it out again because Debi spilled oil on my recipe cards! I had to run like the Road Runner to save them all (beep beep).

It's not exactly the same as when Mom sent it to me. It called for a lot of mustard, and I just don't like mustard. A touch of vinegar gives it a nice flavor. I also added garlic. (I'm part Italian! Garlic is in our blood!) Sometimes I'll use pepperoni instead of sausage, the way I had it at the drive-in once.

You should make this some evening for your other teen-age friends while you listen to records. Invite some boys. Maybe this'll make Bobby Markham sit up and take notice of you!

Hope to see all of you at Thanksgiving.

All my love,

Helen

January 21, 1973
To Debi
From Janie

Dear Debi,

Your dad's lucky to have a good, strong young woman like you while your mom is so sick. You make me proud to be your aunt—but that's nothing new. Here's the recipe you asked for, since you destroyed the original at age nine!

I changed the crust. All the pizzas I've eaten have a yeast-bread crust. That's what the original Italian bakers would use—something they could get their hands into, feel a connection with the earth and life. It's very therapeutic and you should take your time and let your spirit soak it in.

I made this pizza pie several times when I was about your age. I wanted a certain boy to like me, and back then the only thing a girl could do was cook and look pretty. Never did get that boy. I did make it a lot of times for Benny, and the less said about him the better. So my advice is: forget men. Just eat the pizza.

Call if you need anything. I mean it.

Love you,

Aunt Janie

Jim's Pizza

Pizza Crust
1 tbsp. active yeast
1 c. warm water
1 1/2 tbsp. shortening, melted
2 heaping tbsp. sugar
1/2 tsp. salt
3 c. all-purpose flour

Preheat oven to 450 degrees. In a medium bowl, dissolve yeast and sugar in warm water. Let stand until creamy, about 10 minutes.

In a large bowl, mix melted shortening and salt. Add dissolved yeast. Stir in flour. Beat until smooth. Let rest for 5 minutes. Turn dough out onto a lightly floured surface and pat or roll into a round. Transfer crust to a lightly greased pizza pan.

Pizza toppings
2 cans (8-oz) tomato sauce
1 tbsp. sugar
1 tbsp. minced onion
2 tbsp. minced garlic
2 tbsp. white vinegar
1/4 tsp. oregano
1/4 tsp. basil

One roll of pepperoni, sliced thick
2 c. mozzarella cheese

Spread crust with toppings and bake for 15–20 minutes, or until golden brown. Let baked pizza cool for 5 minutes before serving.

July 2, 1982
From Deb
To Brian

Hey Cousin,

Aunt Janie says you're pretty good in the kitchen. As if she'd allow any son of hers <u>not</u> to be. Hey, anytime you want to drop in and cook supper for us, I won't argue. Both of us at work all day, and then I've got to come home and cook . . . Larry's lucky sometimes that he even gets oatmeal. Alicia would probably be happier that way.

Anyway, I found some old letters from around when Mom died. Your mom sent me this recipe for pizza and I made it a lot for Dad. If you're going to be a family cook, you have to make pizza.

If you do it the way your mom likes it, it takes hours. (Aunt Janie talked a lot about soaking up good vibrations but these days I just inhale coffee between daycare and work.) So I also sent you the way I do it just for comparison. Hey, it's not Pizza Hut, but it's supper.

Thought you'd like to know that Alicia can point out "Unca Brine" and "Unca Mart" in pictures. Guess you and Mark made a big impression on her at Christmas! She named her little dog "Pigtails" because of your nickname for her.

Tell Staci I said hello. You two getting married yet?

Your cousin,

Deb

Dad's Pizza

Crust:
1 can refrigerated biscuit dough

Pizza:
1 c. spaghetti sauce
1 tsp. Italian seasoning
2 c. shredded cheese (I buy the pre-shredded stuff—so much faster)
1 pkg. pepperoni

Roll out biscuit dough onto a greased baking pan. Cover with toppings. Bake at 400°F for 10–12 minutes.

September 15, 1989
From Brian
To Mark

Mark,

I meant to get this to you sooner. That's what you get for having a brother who runs a restaurant—I don't have time to send you recipes.

You're lucky Staci's around to stay on my case about things like this.

I'm sending six or seven recipes that should get you set up as a not completely embarrassing excuse for a guy on his own. I can't do anything about your personal hygiene, though.

Be sure you learn the pizza recipe. It's what I cooked for Staci the night I proposed. You remember that night, right? I'd cleaned the apartment, made three personal specialty pizzas, romanced her by candlelight . . . and I was just about to pop the question when you showed up with three horror movies you rented.

You ate an entire pizza (the Mexican one, I think) in the living room and watched people die violently while I was on one knee in the dining room.

I bet you're tired of hearing that story. Tough.

P.S. This uses a pre-made pizza crust, which is probably the best you'll manage with work and school. Once you graduate, I'll show you how to make the real crust, sauce, everything by hand. Then maybe you can be Mom's favorite.

P.P.S. I change this up with different toppings and flavors. I'm sending you the basic recipe.

P.P.P.S. This is why we got you your own VCR that Christmas.

Proposal/Slasher Movie Pizza

Pre-made pizza crust

1/4 cup diced onion

4 cloves garlic, minced *(NOT BULBS! Made this mistake once)*

1 cup sauce*

1 cup shredded mozzarella cheese
Hot pepper flakes (to taste)

Heat oven to 400°F. Sauté onion and garlic in oil until browned, about 3 minutes. Add sauce and toppings of your choice (see options below). Top with cheese and pepper flakes to taste. Bake 20 minutes or until edges are golden brown.

*Sauce suggestions

Heat together:

Traditional: marinara sauce, 1 tsp ground basil, 1/2 tsp ground oregano, 1/2 cup Parmesan cheese. Top with pepperoni or sausage.

Mexican: taco sauce, 1 tsp chili powder, 1 tsp cumin, 1/8 tsp cayenne pepper. Top with ground beef or chicken cooked in taco seasoning.

Chinese: sweet-and-sour sauce, 2 Tbs soy sauce, 1/4 tsp ground ginger. Add 1/4 cup cooked cubed chicken to sauce and heat through. Top with water chestnuts and crunchy noodles. *(Yeah, yeah, Ramen)*

(Note: Use the sauces and toppings sparingly; too much and it gets soggy. Try serving that to your girlfriend, and you'll be watching bad horror movies all alone for the rest of your pathetic life.)

———————

May 30, 2005
From Mark
To Alicia

Hey Pigtails,

Does that husband of yours know that nobody in your family uses your real name? When I saw your wedding invitation I was like who the heck is Alicia? Don't you mean Pigtails? Just kidding. It was a beautiful wedding, and you got a good guy.

So us uncles wowed the rehearsal crowd with our pizza, didn't we? It's a family tradition from back when your grandpa was young. I guess I can send you the recipe now. But I hope you know I had to fight six ninjas and disarm three bombs to get to the vault where we keep it.

Don't tell anybody how easy this recipe is; it's way more fun to show up like heroes with ten handmade pizzas.

Love you,

Uncle Mark

June 12, 2005
From Alicia
To House&Home

Dear House&Home,

Enclosed is my entry for your 50th-Anniversary Family Favorites recipe contest. This pizza has been in my family for generations; my uncles made it for my wedding rehearsal dinner! I "freshened up" their recipe by making my own sauce, and using fresh basil. I also make a hand-tossed crust, with whole wheat for added nutrition. I think it's probably closer to how my great-grandmother (my namesake) would have made her pizza! I hope you enjoy.

Sincerely,

Alicia Ames

The Family Pizza

Crust:
2 cups all-purpose flour
1 cup whole-wheat flour
1 tsp salt

1 cup warm (110°F) water
1 Tbs granulated sugar

1 0.25-oz package active dry yeast
2 Tbs olive oil

Preheat oven to 400°F. Combine flours, salt, sugar, and yeast in a large bowl. Mix in oil and warm water. Knead until soft and elastic; let rest 15 minutes. Spread out on a large pizza pan.

Sauce:
2 garlic cloves, minced
1/4 white onion, minced
1 8-oz can tomato sauce
1/2 tsp vinegar
1 Tbs sugar
1/4 tsp dried basil
1/4 tsp dried oregano

Sauté garlic and onion in olive oil until tender. Add sauce, vinegar, sugar, basil, and oregano. Heat through. Spread on unbaked crust.

Topping:
1 cup chopped fresh basil
1 cup grated mozzarella
1 cup pepperoni (optional)

Bake in preheated oven for 16–20 minutes until crust is golden brown.

Enjoy this authentic family favorite of ours!

The end

The Secret Life
of Paige Parker

The Director's holographic image was distorted—probably on purpose. Headquarters didn't do anything by accident. "You've got your assignment, Agent. This group is the elite of the elite. Don't make us sorry we let you in."

"Don't worry, ma'am," Agent Parker said, pulling on her black jacket. Her shining brown hair fell smoothly down her back. "I'll make it your best unit."

The Director allowed a faint smile to cross her severe lips. "You're pretty confident for somebody who hasn't met her team yet."

Agent Parker flashed her trademark dimpled grin, the one that put her opponents off guard. They never saw her trademark roundhouse kick coming. "You built this team, Director. I figure you know how to do your job."

"You make it easy for us, Agent."

"You're making me blush."

"Blush on your own time." But the Director smiled again. "Headquarters out."

The hologram faded away. With a soft hum, the entire communications console folded in on itself to take the shape of an antique dresser. The holoport flipped over to reveal a mirror in an ornate frame.

Agent Parker reached for her red felt fedora, but it wasn't in its usual spot . . .

. . . "Mama! Mama, look! I gots your hat!"

Paige Parker glanced in the mirror of her grandmother's dresser. Her four-year-old, Gabe, stood mostly naked behind her. He wore her red baseball cap pulled down over his eyes, so all she could see was his dimpled grin.

"Why don't you have any clothes on?" Paige took the cap off his head and clapped it onto her short brown hair. Today's summer humidity meant that it was officially a hat day.

"I lost my shorts," Gabe said. "Adele took them."

"Why would Adele take your shorts? At least go find a shirt!"

Adele *had* taken the shorts. She'd collected three blankets, two shirts, and Gabe's shorts in a cardboard box to make a bed for her baby dragon. "I was just pretending," she explained sheepishly, as if five years of age was a little old to be babysitting an imaginary dragon.

"Pretending is fine," Paige said as she dressed Gabe. "But not right now! Didn't I say we were going to the park? Go see if Emmy found her shoes."

Of course Emmy couldn't find her shoes—this being the child who could spot a sliver of onion in half a pound of hamburger. Paige couldn't find them either; she rustled up an old pair of Adele's sandals with one strap held on by duct tape.

Paige skipped changing Isaac's diaper and gave Gabe's brown hair an ineffectual swipe with a brush. "Okay, that'll have to do. Out to the van."

The park was five miles away, or, as Paige thought of it, one and a half tracks on the *Kid Krooners* CD. She always tried to get to the park before she had to hear that stupid monologue in the middle of "Twinkle, Twinkle Little Star," but this time she didn't make it. "Oh, star, you make the dark night better, like a happy letter, like a friendly Irish setter." Someone actually wrote those lines and thought, *Yeah, this will work!*

Paige pulled into the gravel lot just as her phone beeped with a notification . . .

. . . Paige Parker, CEO of the biggest music label on the East Coast, stepped out of her limousine. Her entourage followed, all immaculate from their perfectly styled hair to their polished shoes. Paige herself wore her trademark red cloche hat around her close-cropped brown hair. She looked cool and poised despite the June humidity.

A hush had fallen over the bystanders. Ignoring their stares—Paige was pretty used to them—she

43

swept up the sidewalk to the soaring glass and steel building that bore her name and logo. *Parker Music.* Only the best, and everybody knew it.

As she walked through the door, a reporter hurried forward to meet her. "Ms. Parker, could you talk to me about your decision to pull the new album of children's songs from the market?"

"It didn't meet our standards," Paige said shortly.

"Rumor says that you didn't like some lyrics written by the producer's seven-year-old kid."

"Ex-producer," Paige said.

"But it was poised to be a huge seller, just like all your others. Wouldn't you say it was a drastic action?"

"I don't compromise. Hundreds of mothers in minivans thank me."

A hand on her shoulder distracted her. She turned to see her private secretary, who slipped her a note. "From . . . you know who."

Paige crumpled the note in her hand and raised her voice. "I'm not available right now. Please make an appointment to see me." She strode to the glass elevator. It sped seventeen stories above the jostling crowd. As it slowed at her private floor, she unfolded the note. Her mind was flooded with the memory of broad shoulders and hungry blue eyes. *Last night was fantastic. You make me crazy. Do we need anything from the grocery store?* . . .

. . . Ahead of Paige, Adele and Gabe ran along the cracked walkway to the playground. Isaac kicked his feet, protesting the stroller. Emmy hung onto the diaper bag on Paige's shoulder, demanding snacks.

Paige balanced her phone on the stroller to read her husband's text. She had to think a moment to remember "last night," since two feedings, an early-rising toddler, breakfast for four kids, and a park trip had happened since then. She slid her finger awkwardly along the digital keyboard.

Serves you right you make me crazy too. Apple juice yogurt bread.

Matt's reply came quickly: *Is yogurt bread near the deodorant pads?*

Paige grinned. Early in their marriage, she'd been shy about sending her new husband to shop for her personal needs. She'd written a list hurriedly, all on one line. Matt returned home frustrated after having looked all over the store and even asked an employee where the "deodorant pads" were. Funny to think those things were once a big deal.

She texted back, *It's near the free babysitters.*

Ok, I'll grab a unicorn while I'm at it.

No good they only like virgins.

Paige wondered what she and Matt would do when Adele started reading fluently and might see their texts. Seemed like a compelling argument against pushing Adele to read too young.

Paige gave Emmy a cracker, then glanced around the playground. It wasn't crowded—just a group of five moms clustered around a picnic table behind the swings. Paige pushed the stroller across the mulched ground toward them. "Are you with the Central Mom's Club?"

"That's us!" said a woman with almond-shaped eyes and a river of sleek, dark hair. Paige felt dowdy with her short brown hair and cap.

But she smiled, because at least she had a dimple. "Oh, good. My email said that I'd been assigned to your playgroup."

"Yes, you must be Paige! I'm Brianne."

The other women introduced themselves in a flurry of names: Heidi, Amanda, Janelle, and Kate.

Kate was very pregnant; she sat on a bench with a young girl between her knees, handing out pretzels with experienced abandon. "I saw you get here. I told everybody you were here to join us."

Paige laughed. "I showed up with four kids under the age of six. I wasn't exactly undercover."

"You and me both," Kate agreed. "Next month I'll have three under five." She pointed at the woman whose auburn hair fell in tight ringlets. "But Janelle has *twins* and a toddler."

"I pretty much went crazy three years ago," Janelle said wryly, leaning against the handle of a side-by-side double stroller where two babies slept. A chubby, red-haired little boy sat at the table drinking a juice box.

"We aren't *crazy*," Brianne corrected. "We're investing in our children. Okay, let's talk play dates for the summer! I'm pretty much wide open—Jeff just left for an extended job, so I'm filling up a lot of time."

"How long is he gone this time?" Kate asked.

"Four weeks initially. We'll see from there."

"Four weeks?" Paige imagined a month apart from Matt, on her own with the four kids. "I admit it. I'd cry every day."

"You get used to it," Brianne shrugged. She opened a spiral-bound daily planner. Her blue pen matched her sapphire ring. "Okay, ideas?"

Paige dropped out of the conversation to put Emmy on a swing, but she caught snatches: "I can plan a craft time for the kids" . . . "We should have some physical activity for rainy days."

"And it would be fun to have a snack-time picnic," Heidi said. She had a long chin and slender, elegant fingers. "I could bring one of my big quilts."

"Heidi makes amazing quilts," Kate said to Paige.

"I'll have to bring Coraline's snacks so she'll have something to eat," said Amanda. She appeared to be older than the rest of the women, judging from the fine lines around her eyes.

"Kids are so picky," Paige said in an attempt to join the discussion. "My kids basically live on mac and cheese and pizza."

Amanda gave a tight smile. Paige suddenly realized she hadn't included a vegetable.

Wails broke out from the play equipment, and Paige sighed. Gabe's voice could summon demons. She trotted to the slides. Heidi was behind her.

Evidently Gabe had lingered at the bottom of the slide, and Heidi's daughter had dive-bombed him. Paige looked him over quickly. "You're not bleeding."

Heidi examined her daughter's cheek carefully. "It's a little bump. I don't think it's too bad." She poured some water from a bottle onto her smooth hand and dabbed it on her daughter's cheek.

Gabe stopped crying to watch. Noticing his interest, Heidi applied the cure to his back where her daughter's head had hit him. He then requested some on his arm, his neck, and a scab on his leg. After a few moments, the crisis was past.

"I'm going to have to remember that one," Paige said. "Miracle water."

"It's really the sympathy they want," Heidi smiled.

"I only have a limited amount of that," Paige said.

"But they're only small once, right?"

"So I hear. How many kids do you have?"

Heidi hesitated, then said, "You met Maisie. You have four?"

"Yes. Pretty much all I can handle," Paige said. Heidi didn't respond. Paige searched for some way to fill up the awkward moment. "So you sew quilts? I can make curtains, but that's about it."

"Mostly baby quilts. I like it. It's . . . therapeutic."

Paige thought about saying that half a bottle of wine after supper was therapeutic, too, but Heidi didn't seem to have the right sense of humor for it. Besides which, Paige didn't actually drink very much.

Back at the picnic table, Paige checked on Isaac and gave Emmy another few pushes on the swing. Brianne updated them: "Okay, so we've got crafts, snacks, and physical activity."

"I thought we were just going to get together and let the kids play," Paige said.

"Oh, sure," Brianne agreed, her ring flashing in the sunlight. "Definitely some free play. But we also want some structure. We need to be *intentional* about focusing on our children instead of getting lax now that it's summer . . ."

. . . One little band of brave warriors did not get lax even when the battle was hot against them. Where the fighting was fiercest, there stood the Lady Pa'Ige, her once-dimpled smile lost in the grime and blood of war. Her sapphire-hilted sword flashed in the sun as she felled her opponent.

Too tired to savor the shred of victory, the Lady closed her eyes in a brief moment of rest.

"My lady!" The wail came above the noise of war around them. Pa'Ige opened her eyes to see Bri rushing toward her. Her once-shining hair fell in limp strings around her weary face. "My lady, we have need of you. It's Hei'Di. She is badly wounded. We are afraid . . ."

Without a word, Pa'Ige sheathed her sword and turned to follow Bri. They ran across the uneven ground to the makeshift hospital tent. Inside, the Lady found Hei'Di lying on an old quilt, her eyes closed and her slender, elegant fingers still.

Three others stood around the body. They raised their eyes when Pa'Ige walked in, silently imploring her to save their companion.

Pa'Ige dropped to her knees and quickly examined the fallen warrior. "Very little blood. Where is water?"

"We have but a little left."

"Give it to me."

They handed her a small stone bottle. Pa'Ige poured its contents out into her smooth hand. Outside the tent, the roar of battle raged on. Pa'Ige said shortly, "I must be alone."

The warriors bowed their heads and filed out of the tent.

Pa'Ige whispered her magic over the lukewarm pool of water in her palm. She had only a limited amount, but it must be enough.

Outside the tent, no one knew how she struggled. Bri said admiringly, "The Lady is made of steel. She and the valiant Prince Matthew have been parted these three years. Yet when I showed pity, she but said, 'You grow accustomed.'"

"She is a marvel of courage," another nodded. "I down a bottle of wine every night just to sleep, but not the Lady. She says that these days will not last."

"Won't they?" Bri said wearily. "What else is there for us, but this great battle?"

"It must be one of her great magic arts to see beyond this battle."

"If only we too had that sight."

A voice from within the tent interrupted their discourse. The Lady called to them. "Come see your companion, my brave warriors."

With joy, they crowded into the tent. Hei'Di was sitting up, the color returned to her cheeks. She cast a grateful look at Lady Pa'Ige. "I cannot ever repay you."

"I need no thanks," Pa'Ige replied, pushing her red helmet from her face. "Just a little rest for all of us—that is what my weary soul longs for." In the distance, they heard the wail of a child . . .

. . . Janelle's twins were stirring; the one on the right was fussing. She sat down at the picnic table and dug around in her diaper bag for two bottles. "Did all of you get my email about a babysitting switch-off?"

Paige perked up.

"There are six of us now," Janelle went on, pulling her auburn hair out of a baby's fist, "so if four of us watched all the kids, two of us could go out for a couple of hours. If we did it once a week, all of us would get a turn pretty soon."

"Free babysitting?" Paige said. "Seriously?"

"Well, tradeoff babysitting, but . . . yeah."

"You know I'm in," Kate said. "I'll take two hours to myself even if I'm in labor."

But Heidi and Amanda looked at Brianne, who frowned.

"I did get the email, Janelle. I'm not sure that would work." She tapped her pen on her planner. "We'll probably need everyone to stay and be involved."

Heidi said, "Maisie is starting preschool in the fall, and this is our last summer together like this."

"You've always got next summer," Paige said, trying not to sound impatient.

At the same time, Amanda put a hand on Heidi's shoulder. "How old would Evan be now?"

Heidi played idly with the cap of her water bottle. "Almost two." She glanced at Paige. "I never know how to answer how many kids I have. It's easier to just say Maisie, but I had Evan too. He came at twenty-eight weeks, and he lived for three days. That's why I make quilts now—for the babies in NICU."

"Oh," Paige said, and brushed the top of Isaac's fuzzy head.

Amanda spoke up. "And until I get Coraline's allergies under control, I think I need to stay with her. She's allergic to dairy, gluten, nuts, and citrus." She put her head in her hand. "I seriously don't know what I'm going to feed her."

"No mac and cheese or pizza. Paige's kids would starve," Kate said with an amused look at Paige.

Paige smiled awkwardly. *Urgent memo to HQ. Your best agent has repeatedly made a fool of herself. Please get her out of here.*

Brianne picked up her pen. "Anybody up for researching some craft ideas?"

"How about *Fun things to do while Mommy's peeing for the seventy-eighth time today*?" Kate suggested, standing up. "It's what pregnant women do. Oh, hey, I have to go to the bathroom."

Paige saw her chance to escape. She checked Isaac's diaper and was glad to find it soaked. "I need to change him. Probably Emmy too. Come on with me, Em."

Janelle turned to her red-haired toddler. "Henry, do you need to go potty?"

The bathrooms were in an outbuilding at the bottom of a gentle slope. Kate, Janelle, and Paige started off in a jumble of strollers and children. As they walked away, Brianne said, "Amanda, do you think you could teach some kid-friendly yoga?"

Kate laughed and shook her head. "Brianne."

Paige cleared her throat. "I'm really not sure I'm the right fit for this group."

"Why not?" Kate exclaimed. "It's a great group!"

"Yeah, but . . . themed snack time and yoga?"

"Oh, don't let Brianne scare you off," Kate said. "She's got great ideas and she lives by that planner. But it always falls apart when we try it with the kids. We really just let them run around and play while we talk. Best of both worlds."

Janelle looked thoughtful. "I think Brianne is trying to keep her head above water. I get the idea that her marriage maybe isn't doing so great. She's the one who should jump on this babysitting tradeoff."

"She won't unless it's her idea, though," Kate said.

"I know. I'm not trying to take things over. It just seemed like we could fit in some coffee time."

Paige said, "Well, there might be a way . . ."

. . . The three revolutionaries walked down the hill to their secret meeting place. Although they wore the same uniform as all the other members of The Society, their squared shoulders hinted that they didn't quite conform.

"We're not trying to overthrow anything," said Agent Parker, adjusting her trademark red cap over her steely eyes. "We're a covert inner operation. We'll meet every Tuesday."

"Yes. Ten o'clock," Janelle agreed, her blazing hair an expression of the fire that burned in her. "But it will take all three of us to make it work."

Kate glanced over her shoulder. "We've got to keep it quiet. If The Society finds out that we're getting away, even for an hour . . ." She trailed off, her arms cradling the child within her.

"Don't worry," said Agent Parker, her dimple flashing briefly in a determined smile. "I see it all now. This is why I was assigned here."

And in her mind, she saluted the Director at Headquarters.

The end

The Dang Truck

I said, "Hunter's, like, part rabbit."

It was Easter. Me and my sister-in-law was cleaning her kitchen up while our husbands let the kids hunt eggs outside. Linzey looked confused, I guess because she was thinking of the Easter Bunny. I didn't mean the Easter Bunny.

"So we get home from church," I explained, "and he drops the kids in front of a video and drags me back to the bedroom. I was like, 'Baby, we got to leave in an hour and one of the kids'll come in!' But he goes, 'Nah, it won't take long. Just got to have some of you before we go.' Like he ain't going to last through Easter dinner at his brother's house!"

Linzey laughed and dried a colander. "Honey, Colt's the same way. I barely got my clothes back on before y'all rang the doorbell. Welcome to the family."

I liked that "welcome" part. Me and Hunter had been married for five years, but sometimes it was still kind of hard to believe I ended up in a good place. I mean, we didn't have any kind of easy life, but it was a dang sight better than what I come from.

But all I said to Linzey was, "Well, I guess we both got to put quarters in the box today."

"I done upped ours to a dollar. I'm aiming for a cruise by next summer."

"Really?" I scraped out a bowl of mashed potatoes. "Hey, maybe if we did that we'd pay off the Dang Truck."

Linzey rolled her eyes. "Yeah, and next thing you know, Hunter will show up with a new boat. He'll be like, 'Hey baby, let's pay this one off with sex, too!'"

"Crap, you are so right. Only quarters in our box."

Linzey and Colt's box was this shiny copper thing with a lid and everything. When I told Hunter about the whole idea (I got it from Linzey), he drug out this old crooked pine box he made with his grandpa when he was eleven. I said maybe it ought to be fancier, but he said it needed to be real sturdy with all the money he expected to put in it. He wasn't wrong.

The kitchen door opened. Five kids and two dogs swarmed into the house. Hunter and Colton come in on their heels. Me and Linzey's conversation was shot to hell; even the dogs had something to say.

I scooped up my little girl, Brailee, and found out her diaper stunk something awful. "Ain't you got a nose?" I asked Hunter.

"Why you think I brung her in?" Hunter grinned. "She don't let me change her anyway."

Colton raised his eyebrows. "You even tried more than twice?"

"Nah. Why fix what ain't broke?"

Colton looked aggravated, which was what Hunter was aiming for. He had changed Brailee more than twice. And he helped me potty-train Branley because he made such a big deal out of "doing it like a man." But he liked getting under his big brother's skin. Colton thought Hunter didn't act like his age or something.

Me, I liked how Hunter was a lot of fun— because truth to tell, our life could use it.

Brailee waved two pink plastic eggs in my face as I laid her on the couch. "Did you hunt them eggs?" I asked.

"Des," she said, smiling her six-tooth grin. I cleaned her up quick—I was real fast at diapers. Then I wrapped the dirty one up tight and put it in the diaper bag.

Hunter said, "You ain't taking that with us?"

"Yeah. Linzey ain't used to stinky diapers in her house no more." Linzey's youngest was six. But me, I had Brailee in diapers, plus I babysat three extra kids every week. One more diaper didn't make no difference when we about drowned in them.

"It'll stink up the whole truck."

"You'd rather it stink up our house than your truck?" Colton said. "When in the heck are you going to grow up, boy?"

"Shut up, Colt, nobody asked you."

I still got kind of nervous when the brothers got after each other, but Linzey just rolled her eyes. "Makayla, throw it in the can out back."

"Throw it at the Dang Truck!" Colton said. Hunter made sure no kids was looking and flipped his brother off.

Hunter loved that Dang Truck. I was eight months pregnant with Brailee when he come driving up in that red monstrosity. I nearly went into labor then and there. He thought I was excited.

When I stopped pitching dishes around the kitchen, I said to him, "Honey, you see a truck that makes your balls tingle. I see a chunk of money every month that we can't afford!" He really was kind of sorry. Turns out we could afford it, when I started babysitting.

(I called it the Damn Truck until Branley got old enough to repeat it at church, so it got to be the Dang Truck.)

I set Brailee on her feet. "We got to get home because Hunter's working tonight."

We loaded up the two kids, then me and Linzey found spots for the leftovers under the seats. Colton walked past and patted Linzey's butt. Hunter pinched mine.

Linzey looked at me and said, "Another quarter for your box before he goes into work, bet you anything."

"Yeah, and I guess you're getting another dollar once we leave."

"Ain't we supposed to be rich by now?" Linzey said.

Hunter overheard that part. "We got to find the leak in our money tank. No matter how much we fill it up, it runs out before the end of the month."

I was glad Linzey had something to say, because my stomach seized up and I was afraid Hunter would notice the look on my face. He didn't. I was leaning over so I guess he looked down my shirt instead.

We hugged about a million times and climbed into the truck. The family was always up in each other's business, but they never let anybody leave without a real goodbye.

Branley was mashing his face against his window making faces at his cousin. "Stop that!" Hunter barked.

"Gage is making faces back at him," I cut in.

"He's smearing snot all over the glass."

"It ain't snot," Branley said, wiping at the spit with a dirty finger.

"Now I got to wash it before I go into work. Stick your tongue out without licking the glass."

Branley did, all the way down the driveway till we turned onto the highway.

Both kids was asleep when we pulled up to our trailer. Hunter parked under the whatever, the canopy. That's where we kept our mower and axe and toolbox and stuff. It's also where we used to park the Honda, but now we put it under the oak tree next to the canopy.

I said, "After you clean that window, you can clean the car's windshield. Got bird crap and leaves all over it."

"Don't know why I should clean it if you ain't never going to drive it."

"I got five kids all on my own every day," I pointed out. "I can't go nowhere."

"You won't drive anyway."

"I drive if I got to."

"Don't see what your deal is. You wasn't even hurt. He deserved it."

"It scared me, okay? I was only sixteen. Just clean the windshield for me, honey."

Hunter unbuckled Branley and picked him up like he didn't weigh nothing. I was trying to unbuckle Brailee without waking her up, but I got distracted by Hunter's arms. That's kind of how me and him got started in the first place. He liked to come to the restaurant where I worked, and pretty soon I figured out it wasn't for the fries. He hung around one night till I got done with my shift, and my ex decided to show up and push me around some. So Hunter flexed them muscles and pushed Dub around—it only took once—and Dub about peed his pants and left. After that, me and Hunter was a couple. All these years later, Hunter's arms still did it for me.

We got the kids to bed without them waking up, then snuck back to our bedroom and tried for another quarter in the box. But we fell asleep. Hunter woke up with just enough time to clean the window of the truck before he headed out, leaving me to make it to bedtime with two tired-rotten kids.

That was pretty much how every day went, holiday or not. He worked days as a Wal-mart mechanic and nights at Boyce's grocery store. I babysat every weekday. We barely had what we needed to pay off the trailer, the bills, our beat-up Honda Civic, and that shiny Ford truck.

And the "leak in the money tank" sure didn't help none.

It was Tuesday afternoon before I got outside to clean the bird crap off the car. Pretty much anything with the car, I had to do.

The kids was playing in the little fenced-in yard a few feet away while I worked. It was a real warm, quiet day and I was enjoying it till I heard a car drive past real slow. We lived down a dirt road, with a few houses farther down. No surprise that somebody would drive past. But I edged around the oak tree to take a look.

A blue Mustang was creeping around the curve past our driveway.

I grabbed up the baby from the playpen and herded the rest of the kids inside. They all pitched fits, but I shouted at them to hush up and I'd put on a video for them. The baby was still wailing when I put her in the swing, but the others climbed up on the couch. I put on a long video. Then I dug in my purse and found the week's grocery money.

I looked out the front door. Prayed he'd just go on past this time. Sometimes he did, if he thought it was too close to when Hunter would come home.

The Mustang showed back up and pulled into our driveway. Dub wasn't driving, of course. Some blond thing—I forget her name—was the one he lived off of right now. He got out of the car, grinning and rubbing the back of his neck. I come out onto the front stoop.

"Hey, Mack. How you doing? That church boy treating you right?"

I didn't answer. I just held out the money.

He walked over to the steps. He was looking old. I guess he always should of looked old to me, considering he was twenty-six when he married me and I was seventeen. But he sure was ragged and sorry these days.

"You got what you want. Go away," I said.

He took the cash and counted it out. Then he gave me this real big pout. "This all? Mack, honey, I need more than this. You know I can't hold a job with my neck and back like it is."

"You leave or I'll call Hunter."

Dub took a step back, but he still grinned at me. "You'll call him and tell him you're giving his money away? To pay up for nearly killing somebody?"

"You didn't nearly die," I said, but I felt my voice kind of shake.

"Still messed up from it though." Dub rubbed his neck again. "Don't worry, Mack. I ain't never told nobody. Well, I told Monica, but she's nice, she won't say nothing."

I looked over at the blond thing driving the Mustang. She raked her eyes over me like I was something they found on the laundry room floor.

"But I need more than this. When you get paid for keeping all them kids?"

"None of your business."

"Sure is a good thing nobody knows about that night, huh? Wouldn't be good for babysitting."

My fingernails was digging into my own hands, I was clenching my fists so hard. "Get out of here, you bastard."

"I thought you gave up cussing since you married that church boy."

"I did, but God thinks you're a bastard too."

Dub laughed. "Thursdays. I remember now, you get paid on Thursdays. See you Friday, sweetheart."

He got back in the car. Blond Thing wheeled around and spun out of the driveway. Gravel popped against the old Honda.

I was used to Dub showing up every once in a while. It always got my heart to racing and made it hurt to breathe. I made it through the rest of the day okay by burying him under all my other thoughts. God knows I was tired enough to forget about anything.

That evening, Hunter was looking in the fridge and said, "We're out of milk. And beer. And bread. Pretty much everything."

"Get a carrot," I said.

"When we going grocery shopping?"

I was glad I was washing dishes so I didn't have to look up. "We can go tomorrow night. But . . . we need to use the credit card."

"What for? We got cash last week."

"It just goes so fast. Sorry."

"What the heck happens to it? You never even go nowhere."

Something about his words just touched off a fuse. I whipped around and started yelling. "How can I? I got to stay here and make money! You can get in your shiny damn truck anytime you want to, and you're complaining?"

I was sorry as soon as the words left my mouth. I didn't mean to blow up all over him. He looked real shocked. He slammed the fridge shut and went storming outside.

I felt pretty rotten. Later he come back in, and I said I was sorry. When we went to bed, I dressed up for him and made it real good. Apparently it worked; he put two quarters in the box.

"It's getting pretty full," he said as we settled down to sleep. "I counted it a couple of days ago, and we got something like fifty dollars in there."

"Should we put it toward the credit card?"

"No," Hunter grunted. "We ain't paying a credit card out of our box. You be thinking of something special you want to do."

It made me giggle; I couldn't help it. I remembered the last "something special" from the box. It was one of them times when there wasn't nothing fun to do, so Hunter made fun up.

He come home from work that evening and was like, "Get the kids, get in the truck, we're going out."

We dropped the kids off at Colton and Linzey's. While he took the kids' car seats out of the truck, I asked, "So what now?" There wasn't nowhere to go in our town but McDonald's and Hardee's.

Hunter said, "Just a little fun."

We drove fifteen miles to the next town. Hunter pulled into an empty parking lot, right next to the sign that said: Grace Baptist Church. *When God says it, do it!*

He pulled out a couple of fancy glasses we got as wedding presents. He had a couple bottles of Coke, a box of chicken nuggets for each of us, and some of them Star Crunch cookie things, my absolute favorite snack.

After we ate, he said he figured nobody would pay attention to a truck if it was parked by a church sign. So we jumped into the empty back seat. We had ourselves a good time, with the radio going and traffic speeding past on Highway 11. It was the only time I loved that Dang Truck.

So lying in bed with him, I fell asleep with his big arm slung over me, thinking how much he could do with fifty dollars.

*

I didn't forget Dub said he'd come back. He just stayed buried in my head. When Jess, who I babysat for, asked if she could pay me Monday instead, I didn't even think. I just said that was fine.

Friday morning about ten o'clock I heard a car in the driveway. I thought Jess come back or something. But when I looked, there was a blue Mustang, shining so bright in the sun it hurt my eyes.

I went for my purse but remembered I didn't have no money. My throat kind of closed up. Out the window, I seen Dub coming up to the front door.

Suddenly Branley was right there with me, looking out the window. "There's that mean man," he said. "He's scary."

"Back up!" I snapped. "Get away from the window! You stay away from the window and don't come outside, you hear me?"

Then I went out onto the stoop. Dub stopped at the bottom step. "I'm in a hurry," he said.

"I ain't got nothing."

"What?"

"Didn't get paid."

This time, Dub wasn't grinning. His eyes got real narrow, and he licked his lips. "It ain't an option, Mack. I came for money."

"You'll have to come back another time."

He started up the steps. It had been a long time since he laid a hand on me—but not so long that I forgot what it was like. He stepped real close. The smell of him, beer and cigarette smoke and that one kind of soap he liked, made me sick. "A couple hundred dollars is all it'd take to make me go away. Hell, I'd take fifty this time. Just to remind you that you don't tell me no."

His eyes shifted past me. "That your young'un?" I turned to see Brailee at the window in nothing but a diaper. "Little girl? Pretty little thing."

My chest felt tight, like it was too small for me. "I . . . might have something. You stay right here."

He folded his arms. His eyes was still narrow.

I slammed the front door and locked it and run down the hall to our room. I grabbed the box with two hands.

It was so heavy I couldn't hardly budge it. I stuck my hands into it. The coins clinked together, like when Hunter leaned over me, his big chest across mine, to put a quarter in the box.

I took my hands out. All them coins slid back into the box.

I run back into the living room and herded kids into Branley and Brailee's room at the back of the trailer. I told them to keep quiet, which they didn't, but I got them in the room and the baby in the crib. "Y'all stay in here!" I said, shutting the door.

Quick as I could, I run through that trailer and locked the doors and windows. It took maybe a minute, but it felt like an hour.

The guns was locked up tight in our room and I didn't know what to do with one anyway. I grabbed my purse and dumped it out on the floor. My phone went sliding underneath the coffee table.

Dub pounded on the door. "Makayla, you get back out here!"

I was on my knees, scrambling for the phone. "You leave now," I shouted through the door. "I'm going to call the police! Hunter's best friend is a cop—you better be leaving!"

"You come out and give me my money!"

"It's mine! Mine and Hunter's, and you can just go to hell!"

He banged on the door again. Then he went real quiet.

I got the phone, but was shaking too hard to use it. I peeked out the window. He wasn't standing on the stoop no more. I was even more scared not knowing where he was.

I run to look out my bedroom window where I could see the driveway. I hoped Blond Thing was peeling out in her stupid Mustang, but she was still there, sitting in the driver's seat.

She seemed real upset.

I looked where she was looking, and I kind of screamed. Dub was standing under the canopy, and he'd found the axe.

He walked up to the Honda. "You don't say no to me, Makayla!" he shouted so I could hear him. He swung the axe and smashed it right down on the windshield. The glass broke into a billion tiny cracks. "I'll be back, and next time it won't be your car!" He hit the windshield again.

Then he slung the axe at the house. It hit the side with a big blam. He finished off by calling me a stupid bitch and a filthy slut. Then he got in his girlfriend's car and yelled at her, too.

Blond Thing looked like she'd been eating lemons, but she didn't say nothing. Just drove away real fast.

I stood there looking at that wrecked windshield. I couldn't hide this from Hunter no more.

*

Hunter come on home when I said it was an emergency. His big truck whipped into the driveway and stopped in a cloud of dust. He was talking before he got out. "What's wrong? You okay?"

"I'm okay. Nobody's hurt." I should of been a screaming mess, but that would scare the kids. So I kept calm, standing by the car holding the sleeping baby. The other kids was playing in the yard behind me.

I waited for him to notice the windshield, but he kept looking at me. Finally I pointed at the car.

His eyes got real big. "What the hell—" He remembered the kids. "What the heck happened?"

I started to tell him, but as soon as I said "Dub,"
he cut me off. "You been seeing him?"

"Not on purpose!" I shifted the baby to my other
shoulder. "He comes by now and then. For
money."

"I hope you ain't giving it to him!"

"I didn't want to. But . . ."

"You've been giving him money?" Hunter
shouted. I felt like he'd hit me. He glanced at the
kids and quieted down again. "What are you
thinking?"

I wasn't thinking too much, just trying not to
break down. "Well, I mean, he can't work because
of the accident . . ."

"So what? It ain't like you drove him into that
tree—"

I felt cold even though the sun was still pretty
bright. "Yeah, I did."

"You told me . . ."

"I lied. We lied. Heck, we told most people I wasn't even with him that night. I was drunk. He made me hide till the police was gone."

Hunter looked at me like he couldn't figure out what to say.

"So yeah. I'm a liar and I've been stealing money from you to give to my ex." I hugged that baby tight and felt like my sixteen-year-old self again, lost and trapped and so sad.

"Why didn't you tell him to shove off?"

I jerked my head toward the smashed windshield. "I did."

The baby woke up, whimpering. "She needs to be changed." I waited a minute or two, but Hunter wasn't looking at me no more. So I turned around and walked up the steps to the front door.

Hunter got in his truck and drove away.

I cried a lot while changing the baby. But turns out if I wanted to feel lonely, I was out of luck. About half an hour later, Colton showed up. He come up on the stoop with a folding chair in one hand and a rifle in the other. "Hunter asked if I'd hang around to make sure nobody comes back," he said. "Don't pay no attention to me."

"Where's Hunter?"

"Sheriff's office. Talking to Joel." Hunter's best friend really was a cop; I hadn't lied about that.

When Jess come to pick up her kids, I wasn't going to say nothing about Dub. But with Colton sitting right there with his gun on his lap, it was kind of hard to not mention it.

"Some crazy guy showed up. Nobody got hurt," was all I said. But I knew the story was going to get around town real fast. Jess loaded up her kids in her minivan, eyeing that broken windshield.

Nothing like working my tail off to support one man, only to get it ruined by another man. Damn men.

I sat Branley and Brailee down to macaroni and cheese. Then I fixed a couple of ham sandwiches with the last of the leftovers from Easter. I took a

plate out to Colton, who asked if I'd heard from
Hunter.

That minute my phone rang. "Guess I'm about
to," I said. "Hey, about time you called."

"Everything okay?" Hunter asked.

"Yeah, Colt's here. Where you at?"

"Sheriff's office. Got something to tell you."
Hunter sounded funny, I couldn't really tell why.
"I come down here to report Dub, had to wait
around for Joel to get back from a call. He hauled
in some guy for threatening a cashier at that gas
station out on Fireman's Road, you know the
one?"

"I guess so," I said.

"So I was there when they brung him in. I saw
who it was."

Suddenly I realized why Hunter sounded weird.
He was laughing. "Guess who? Good old Dub. His
girlfriend dropped his sorry ass off at the edge of
town and drove away."

"Oh. Oh, wow." I reported to Colton, "They got him."

Hunter was still talking. "He was drunk as hell, of course. Laid eyes on me and just lost it. Going on about how you ruined his life. See, you made him mad and apparently his girlfriend didn't like what she seen. I mentioned our car, said he had a damn fine swing for somebody with a bad back. He didn't want to talk about that. But he did say how it's your fault he can't get a job."

"Oh no . . ."

"Well, he shut up real quick when I pointed out he let a sixteen-year-old girl drive drunk and then made her hide from the police. He's lucky it was so long ago. He's in such a crapload of trouble already."

Hunter was laughing again. "His girlfriend didn't even leave him his phone. He'd still be sitting at that gas station if the cashier hadn't called the cops on him."

I laughed a little bit. Then I felt like I might cry a lot. "Are you coming on home?"

"Yeah, pretty soon."

"Is Dub in jail?"

"Yup, unless he can find somebody to post bail for him. He made too many women mad at him, so he ain't got no money. Hope he rots there." Hunter laughed again. "Everything's okay, Makayla."

*

But it wasn't okay.

Jess mailed me my last babysitting check with a note that said her mom would watch her kids from now on, which I didn't blame her. Who would want to leave their kids with a woman in a trailer who gets her car smashed by ex-husbands? Not me. Not like I had any choice.

I didn't miss babysitting, but I sure missed the money. Hunter worked more hours, but there wasn't going to be enough to fix that car for a while.

Hunter said he was dead tired. Too tired for any kind of fun—even for sex. He hadn't never been too tired for that before, and I thought it had more to do with the kind of wife I turned out to be than the extra work. Didn't blame him neither.

One Saturday between his shifts, Hunter said, "Think you could get another job?"

"I can't do nothing but watch kids. Maybe clean houses. I ain't too good at that, though." Laundry and dishes and toys and junk was everywhere. "Besides, I'm stuck at home because the car ain't fixed."

At least Hunter didn't give me a hard time about not liking to drive. He leaned his head back on the couch and closed his eyes. "Colt says you ought to take some self-defense classes. That something you'd like?"

"I got no idea," I snapped. "All I ever done is get married and divorced and have babies and make money to pay for stuff."

"Guess that's life," Hunter said. He didn't open his eyes until it was time to leave for work.

The next Monday, Hunter got home early from Boyce's. I was cleaning orange popsicle off Brailee's face when he walked in. "You home already?"

"I took off early," he said. He looked wiped out. "We need to talk."

After the kids were in bed, Hunter sank down on the couch, me next to him. I hoped I didn't look as worried as I felt.

"Here's what I got to tell you." He stared at the blank TV screen. "It's too hard, Makayla. Me working two jobs, the car broke, you not able to do nothing. I'm even too tired to make love. I been realizing I can't handle this no more. It ain't okay."

"What are you saying?" I whispered.

He seemed to have a little trouble answering. Finally he got the words out. "I sold my truck to Joel."

I just stared at him. He thought maybe I hadn't heard him. "Joel needs a new vehicle . . ."

"You sold him the Dang Truck? Why?"

"I told you. I can't take this life no more." Hunter went on to say that he'd still have to work nights a few more weeks—we had a lot of bills to catch up on. And if I could pick up babysitting again for a while, we could use the extra money. Obviously he'd been thinking about it a lot.

Me, I felt kind of shaky. And then the tears started.

He wrapped his big arms around me. "You be thinking about what you want to do. For yourself."

I held onto him. I wasn't sure if I was happy or kind of sad that he got rid of that stupid truck he loved so much. "You're a good man," I said.

"Not really. But at least I tried this time." Hunter kissed me so long I couldn't breathe. I finally pushed him away.

"Okay, Baby. I found a whole dollar in the laundry today. Let's go put it in the box and make it something special."

The end

In a Canoe

Standing at the lodge window, Jordan shaded her eyes against the harsh morning light. The sun on the lake shattered into a thousand tiny shards.

A speedboat bobbed at the end of the pier, overrun with a jumble of people, orange life vests, multicolored swimsuits, and noise. While Randy checked something at the front of the boat, Nina stood in the center of the crowd, giving directions. Her shorts emphasized her generous thighs. She'd stopped caring about her thighs when she turned thirty.

Jordan ran a hand across her black swim shorts. She had very nice legs, she'd been told. Nice hair, too, a dark and glossy complement to her olive skin. Too bad the rest of her was so bland.

She hadn't wanted to come to the lake this year, but Nina had begged her. "Nobody misses the week at the lake!"

"Nobody?"

"Nobody worth mentioning. You can't not come. Curtis came the summer after his accident."

"That's because Curtis never lets anybody down."

"Hey, I don't either! Didn't I come to your swimming party when I had pneumonia?"

"That was in the eighth grade!" But it made Jordan smile. "Okay, I'll come."

She threw herself into the festivities. She helped move tables and set up food stations, kept the lemonade pitcher filled and the beer iced, ate grilled food, stayed up late around the bonfire, and competed in the kayak relay. She smiled a lot. The bustle and noise shredded her nerves, but she didn't show it. No one had any reason to remember that she was alone this year.

But she'd begged off the tubing trip this morning. She watched the speedboat sail toward the little island in the middle of the lake. They wouldn't be back for hours.

Jordan drew a breath of relief as quietness settled around her.

She went into the kitchen and found some hard cider. Alcohol at ten in the morning seemed to suit her mood. As she worked the top off the bottle, the sun streamed through the gauzy curtains, highlighting the wandering black cracks on the old Formica tabletop.

"Hey. Didn't go out with the gang?"

Curtis walked into the kitchen. His reddish hair was wet from a shower.

"I wasn't up to it today. You?"

"Not good for my knee."

"Oh, right." She glanced at his left knee, crisscrossed with white scars.

"I'm taking my canoe out instead."

Jordan nodded and took a sip of the sharp cider. Curtis started some coffee. While it brewed, he opened several plastic containers until he found doughnuts. Jordan took another sip. As much as she liked the idea of drinking the morning away in solitude, the warm scent of coffee enticed her. "Is there enough for me?"

"Sure." Curtis poured her a mug. He held up a jar of powdered creamer. "You still drink it with a pound of this junk?"

Jordan smiled. "Just a couple of tablespoons now. We aren't in high school anymore."

"Over twelve years, can you believe it?" Curtis passed her the box of mini chocolate doughnuts, and she took two.

"Time goes by so fast. Eight months—" Jordan cut off her words.

Curtis took a drink of coffee, not looking quite at her. "Do you ever hear from Dane?"

Of course he knew what was on her mind. Like Nina and Randy, Curtis had been around all through the sublimity and chaos of Dane. "Not really. He was still backpacking through Europe last I knew."

"That's what I heard, too."

"It's what he always wanted to do," Jordan explained, as she did every time. "He saved his money for years to do it. He's going to write a book about it."

"I better get royalties."

"Why?"

"Because he saved a good bit of money by crashing at my apartment for three months."

Jordan knew that. She also knew that Curtis and Dane had had some kind of falling-out. But it was just after the breakup, so she'd never asked for details. "That's just what he does," she said awkwardly. "He hates being tied to one place very long. He's too adventurous. That was part of our problem, actually."

"He has that problem with a lot of people." Curtis finished off his coffee. "Come on, let's go canoeing."

"I'm just going to stay here."

"Oh, come on. It's a perfect day."

Jordan glanced out the window. "It is?"

"And I could use the help rowing—kind of strains my back."

Curtis had broad, straight shoulders, but Jordan knew that his recovery had been a long haul. "Oh, well, I can help out." The lodge really was too quiet, now that she thought of it.

They walked down the sandy lawn to the lake, where Curtis' red canoe sat near the lapping water. Once they were settled in the boat, he gently pushed off.

She expected him to aim for the island, but instead he steered them toward the left shore.

"I've been around most of this lake," he explained. "But there's a little channel I've never explored."

They propelled the canoe with leisurely strokes. Their rhythm felt familiar. They'd canoed together a lot once. That was the summer when Curtis talked about marrying Christine, and Jordan hadn't had much to say about it. She'd never liked Christine much.

As it turned out, Curtis and Christine didn't get married. Then Curtis wrecked his bike off the side of a mountain and tore up his knee and back, and meanwhile Dane—whom Jordan had known since college but never considered before—burst into her life and wrapped her up for two years.

Now here they were. Back in a canoe together on the lake.

They passed houses and waved at people on piers and boats. Then the shore became emptier. The underbrush grew right up to the water— pretending to be a wilderness among these lake homes, Jordan thought with amusement. She snagged a small yellow bloom as they passed a bush, admiring the symmetry of its petals before letting it drift away on the water.

Curtis dragged his paddle through the water lilies, slowing the canoe at the mouth of an unobtrusive channel that emptied into the lake. "This is it."

The channel wound through grass-covered banks and curved out of sight. Jordan's curiosity was piqued. She always wanted to know what was around the next bend. Since Dane never liked to stay in one place very long, they had seemed like the perfect match. Right up until the end of the day, when Jordan was ready to go back home and Dane didn't consider anywhere a home to return to.

"Let's check it out," she said.

The current was gentle, the water just deep enough for the canoe to glide between the narrow banks. As the lake and its tangled memories disappeared behind them, Jordan lost herself in the smooth motion of the canoe, letting green grass and white sand meld with the clear brown of the water. *It's like sailing through a Monet,* she thought. She almost said it aloud, but stopped herself in time.

The channel seemed to end in a swath of tall, slender green reeds. The banks rose higher than their heads. Jordan heard the rush of flowing water beyond the reeds. "A creek runs past here?"

Curtis gazed thoughtfully toward the sound of the water, and Jordan knew he was consulting one of the myriad maps he kept in his head. He had an almost infallible sense of direction. That rainy weekend on the mountain three years ago, when he'd gotten separated from the other cyclists and didn't show back up, no one believed he was lost; they all knew he must be injured.

"That would be the Little Sandy River," Curtis said finally. "I didn't realize it fed into the lake." He brushed a clinging reed from his arm. "What do you think? Do you want to go back?"

Jordan glanced at Curtis's familiar blue eyes and freckled face. "I'm up for going on."

"Let's do it."

As she propelled them forward, he guided them through the reeds. The long leaves left wet stripes on her arms, and the boat disturbed a school of shiny black water bugs. This time she couldn't resist making a remark. "Look at the designs they make in the water while they're running away. Kind of a sad beauty."

"Sad, beautiful bugs?"

Curtis was smiling, but she regretted she'd said it. Dane used to say her comments were "cute." She'd liked it until she suspected he was using it as a synonym for "annoying." She dipped her paddle back into the water and pushed the canoe forward.

They broke free into a tree-shaded river. Jordan kept close to the bank, where the current was slower, while Curtis surveyed the water. "Looks deep enough," he said. "We'll need to watch out, though. Look for where the water flows in a V." He held his fingertips together to demonstrate. "It means there's something under the water. But," he added wryly, "you usually figure it out after you hit it."

"A lot like life," Jordan remarked.

Curtis gave a short laugh. "Unfortunately true."

They paddled into the middle of the river, which welcomed them with a robust current. The water caught the sun in undulating sparkles. A light breeze rustled the trees. It *was* a perfect day, Jordan realized.

Her thoughts drifted with the river. She found herself remembering the day she and Curtis had gone to the county fair together. She had expected him to ask her out afterward, but he didn't. That was the summer he started dating Christine. She was surprised at how fresh the memory seemed.

Curtis's voice broke into her thoughts. "Do you smell popcorn?"

Jordan lifted her nose into the breeze. No wonder she was remembering the county fair. They were surrounded by the sweet, buttery scent of kettle-cooked popcorn.

"Yeah. And do I hear music?"

"I sure do." Curtis turned and pointed over his left shoulder, wincing slightly. "From there."

They angled upstream toward the bank. The music grew louder, and the smell of popcorn blended with frying food. Through the trees, they glimpsed purple, yellow, and blue tents.

"I think it's a craft fair or something," Curtis said.

"We could stop on the sandbar up there and check it out."

"Yeah, sounds good. I need to rest my back anyway."

They pulled the canoe up onto the sandy bank and stowed their paddles. A narrow path led through the trees. It took them up a leaf-scattered slope, and they emerged next to a lemonade booth.

A gravel road ran past, lined on both sides with booths selling crochet, pottery, pies, candy, and wooden toys. At the far end, an energetic country band played on a temporary stage.

"It's like we walked out of the woods into some kind of otherworld bazaar or something!" As soon as she said the words, Jordan cringed inside. She was so *cute*.

Curtis smiled again. "Want some popcorn?"

"Sure."

As they strolled through the crowd, sharing popcorn and lemonade, Jordan again remembered that day at the county fair. "So do you ever hear from Christine?" she asked, running her hand across a rack of knitted scarves.

"Kind of," Curtis replied. "She's married and has a baby. I'm happy for her."

"What . . . went wrong with you two?"

"She had her reasons, I had mine. Basically, we just really didn't belong together."

"So which one of you got to decide that?"

Curtis gave her a sideways glance. "It was a mutual thing."

"Sorry. I really shouldn't have said that." Jordan moved to the next booth, the white gravel dust clinging to her dark legs.

Curtis fell into step with her. "It wasn't mutual with you and Dane, was it?"

"He asked me to go to Europe with him," Jordan said quickly. "I was the one who said no."

"Oh. So it was your fault that you broke up?"
His tone was almost a challenge.

Jordan shrugged. "Not entirely. But . . . he did
give me a chance to make it work."

Curtis seemed about to speak, then didn't after
all. The silence between them stretched a little too
long. Jordan said, "I'm sorry Dane keeps coming
up."

"You don't have to keep apologizing. Especially
not for him."

"I don't know why I can't let it all go . . . I need
to shut up."

Curtis seemed uncomfortable, and Jordan felt
hot and cold all over with embarrassment. "Do you
want to go back to the canoe?"

"Yeah."

The music and smells followed them down the
path. Jordan walked quickly, but Curtis didn't
seem to be in as much of a hurry. He made his way
carefully down the sandy slope, and paused to gaze
upstream.

"We could go a little farther up if you want to," he suggested. "Then we'll just let the river take us back down."

Jordan picked up her paddle, relieved that he wasn't trying to end the outing as soon as possible. "Sounds good."

As they rowed up the river, Jordan found herself staring at the white scars on Curtis's knee. She remembered getting the phone call from Randy: "Good news first—they found Curtis. Bad news, we don't know how bad he is yet." That cold, rainy night, she'd gone to bed scared of waking up to a world with a different Curtis in it.

She forced herself to focus on the river, the breeze, and the chatter of water around her. But the memories had forced open a locked door, and ran rampant over the wilderness Dane had claimed for so long.

The river curved out of sight. Curtis smoothly swung the canoe around. Jordan flexed her arms, glad that the current was working with them now.

Curtis cleared his throat. "You said you couldn't let go."

She met his eyes, startled. He went on, "I understand a little bit. All of us pick up the slack for Dane."

"What do you mean?"

"Well, remember when he took that road trip across the country a few years ago?"

"Yeah."

"He didn't bother to look up hotels, just drove to somebody's town and called them. He's got tons of friends. And we all think, 'Sure, I'll do him this one favor.' You get fifty people doing you a favor each, you can live pretty easy."

"Well, everybody likes him. . ."

"Do you know how he could leave for Europe with just that backpack?"

"How?"

"Most of his stuff is stored at Randy's office. The rest is in my basement. I moved it, because he was hiking on the Appalachian Trail that weekend."

It was exactly something Dane would do. She ventured to ask, "Is that what your fight was about?"

"No. Not exactly." He didn't seem to want to say more.

The river's chatter had become a deep rush, and Jordan absently noticed the water split into three wide, graceful Vs several feet ahead.

Curtis spoke again. "He never takes responsibility. He just expects everybody else to take it for him. I was thinking . . . he left you holding most of the blame. Maybe you need to. . ."

Jordan stiffened. "Watch out!"

The canoe slammed against an underwater log, spun, and hit another one. Jordan's paddle slipped out of her hands. Curtis lunged for it, throwing his weight on his bad knee. A shock of pain crossed his face.

Jordan hooked her left arm around a gray limb jutting up from the water, and stretched out of the boat as far as she could. The paddle bobbed on fast little waves just beyond her fingertips.

The canoe shifted away. She tightened her grip on the slippery wood.

"Let go!" Curtis exclaimed.

"The paddle," she gasped.

"I'll get a new one!"

The canoe rocked precariously, nearly tipping Jordan into the graveyard of trees. Her fingernails dragged along slimy wood as she uncoiled her arm from the limb. She scraped her ribs against the boat as she hauled herself in.

Grabbing the remaining paddle from the bottom of the boat, she thrust it into the water. Curtis straightened up, one hand still cupping his injured knee, and swept his gaze over the river. "Nothing up ahead that I can see."

Jordan steered them toward shallow water. The bottom of the canoe slushed into the gritty riverbed and came to rest on wet sand.

"Are you okay?"

They asked the question at the same time, and both laughed breathlessly.

"How's your knee?"

"Hurts like heck. I need to get back and wrap it. Your arm is bleeding."

Jordan lifted her left arm and found a long, shallow scrape from her wrist to her elbow. Her ribs hurt, and she was covered with mud and bits of waterlogged wood. "I'm sorry."

"For what?" Curtis was leaning over the side of the boat, checking for damage.

"I should have said something sooner."

"It happens." He pulled himself back into his seat.

"I nearly turned us over trying to get that paddle—"

"Jordan. Stop apologizing."

Jordan rinsed her arm in the water. Sudden tears made the sun unusually bright. She wiped them away with the back of her hand. They fell faster.

"I didn't mean to sound so harsh," Curtis said, alarmed. "I just meant . . ."

She covered her face with her hands and sobbed.

After a few moments, Curtis pushed off. The canoe moved swiftly and easily. They weren't fighting the current anymore.

They drifted until her tears finally began to run out. The forward motion of the boat stopped.

And Curtis, in a voice just above a whisper, said, "Jordan? Look."

She opened her eyes to see a yellow and purple flower float past the boat.

She blinked and spotted another bloom, then another. Lifting her head, Jordan saw dozens of flowers and petals dancing on the surface of the water like confetti.

She pushed her hair out of her face and looked around her. Color and bloom exploded in every direction. It took her breath away.

"Where are we?" she asked.

Curtis's voice was still hushed. "I took another little channel. And . . . this is where it led."

The canoe drifted in an almost circular pool. Pansies, daisies, and geraniums rimmed the pool's grassy bank—a riot of vibrant purple, white, pink, and yellow.

A small house was tucked among the far trees, and Jordan's heart warmed toward the unknown gardeners. "They took something ordinary and made it amazing," she said softly.

"Like you do," Curtis said.

She glanced at him and realized she hadn't even worried about sounding cute.

Curtis cleared his throat. "So . . . the fight Dane and I had."

The name gave her a pang, but only a faint one. "What about it?"

"He told me you broke up with him. Made it sound like it was your decision. But Nina told me you were wrecked about it and I got the real story. Of all the idiotic, selfish things he's done, that was the worst. I kicked him out of my apartment. He's not getting any more favors off me."

Jordan spoke thoughtfully. "He *is* the one who broke it off."

"Yeah."

"He knew I wanted a real life together, not just a long backpacking trip. He knew I'd say no." Jordan watched a spindly water spider dash among the floating petals. "You know, he was the one who started our relationship. I was never his type. He must have seen that. Why would he do that?"

She didn't expect a response, but Curtis answered anyway.

"I think it's because you're . . . good for the soul, Jordan. You see wonderful things in life. And life can be hard, and sometimes a man needs a safe haven. And . . ." Curtis stopped. "And I'm not really talking about Dane anymore."

Jordan met his eyes. His face was red.

"I wanted to ask you out years ago. But I was stupid. Afraid you weren't interested. Christine was pretty obvious, so I asked her instead."

"I wanted you to ask me out. I should have said something."

They sat without speaking. The flowers blended into a Monet landscape, and the ripples of the water seemed almost musical.

"Well, since we're confessing," Curtis said awkwardly, "what I really wanted to say this morning was—I'd like to spend some time with you. I know you're not really ready, but when you are, I'm interested in taking things further. Want to go out in the canoe?"

Jordan laughed. "Sure. Want to find a hidden craft fair and eat popcorn?"

"I'd love to. It's a date."

The canoe turned a lazy circle among the bright blooms. Jordan took a deep breath of the flower- and water-scented air. The sun shone like diamonds on the water.

The end

Uncle Bobby's Laying on the Porch

It was a hot spring day in the South. Gloria's recliner sat right beside a window where a popcorn tree grew. The leaves trembled and jittered at the slightest breeze. Even when it was so hot she'd melt except it was so humid she couldn't, Gloria could look at those trembling leaves and pretend there was a high wind.

She had about twenty minutes to pretend to be cool before she had to see about the cake for her friend Marilyn's surprise birthday party tomorrow. Gloria didn't like surprise parties and she didn't like baking cakes, but she liked Marilyn. So when Joan asked her to help out, Gloria agreed.

"By the way," Joan added, "do we know how old Marilyn is?"

"She's about our age."

"Well, how old is that?"

"I don't know. I stopped counting about twenty years ago."

It wasn't really a fib. Sitting in her recliner, Gloria gazed at the framed photo on the opposite wall. Jim smiled back, forever forty-seven. It wasn't that she didn't know her age; it was just that it was difficult to acknowledge that she was so much older than Jim now.

Her thoughts were interrupted by a phone call. She expected it to be her daughter Kristen, who had promised her some tomatoes from her garden. Instead, it was her daughter-in-law, Danielle.

Danielle was forthright and determined, much like a bulldozer. "Gloria! I'm at Uncle Bobby's! You've got to come down here! He's laying down on his front porch and he won't get up."

"He won't . . . ? He what . . . ?"

"He says he's hot and it feels good to lay on the porch."

Gloria's brother was a reclusive bachelor who was generous to a fault—the fault being that he was as obstinate as a brick wall. His nieces and nephews grew up knowing that Uncle Bobby would fix or heal or grow anything. These days the family was always ready to help him out . . . whether he wanted it or not.

"That doesn't sound good," Gloria said.

"I think he's real sick."

"I'm coming."

She was halfway out the door when she caught a whiff of warm chocolate. Darn that cake! Darn Marilyn for having a birthday! Who needed surprise parties at their age, anyway? Liable to give somebody a heart attack.

She took out her phone and texted Kristen on her way out to the car: *When you drop off tomatoes, get cake out of oven.*

Bobby lived three miles away in a little cabin surrounded by pine trees—a setting as reclusive as he was. As she got out of her car, Gloria could see Bobby lying on the porch. Danielle sat next to him.

He was dressed in his usual green cotton shirt and heavy khaki work pants, wearing socks but no shoes. His lined face was pale and drawn. Gloria

mounted the steps and looked down at him. "You
need to go to the doctor."

"No, I'm not going to the doctor."

He was speaking the unsullied truth. He was
half a heel short on his right foot because he'd
refused to have an infection seen to five years ago.

"You're the only brother I've got left. I have to
keep you alive as long as I can," Gloria said,
gripping her hands together until they ached.

Danielle said, "I'm calling Melissa to come out
here."

"Don't go calling Melissa. She'll just bother
me," Bobby grumbled. Danielle was dialing before
he stopped speaking.

As they waited for Melissa, Bobby slipped into
a light sleep. Gloria kept nudging him with her toe
to make sure he wasn't dead. Melissa's black truck
finally crested the hill, and she got out with her
nurse's kit.

"So what's the problem, Uncle Bobby?" she
asked. He opened his eyes.

"Just hot. Laying here to keep cool."

Melissa was easy to please but had a backbone of steel. She was actually from Jim's side of the family, but Bobby was uncle to a lot of extra people.

After taking his blood pressure, Melissa sat back on her heels, frowning. "You're liable to have a stroke pretty soon."

"Well," Bobby conceded, "I guess I'll go to the doctor tomorrow."

Melissa stood up, straightening her steel backbone. "You don't got till tomorrow. You need to go now."

"I can't take you tomorrow anyway," Gloria snapped. "I've got a party to go to."

Faced down by a sister and two nieces, and obviously feeling pretty lousy, Bobby surrendered. He refused to put his shoes on, but allowed himself to be led to Danielle's truck.

"Now, I got to get to work," Melissa said. "Don't you die on the way to the ER."

"If I do, it's because y'all are dragging me around like a sack of turnips," Bobby muttered. "And speaking of, I got to get back this evening. Got a whole row of turnip greens that'll burn up in this heat if I don't pick them."

Gloria replied sarcastically, "I'm sure they'll be fine if they just wait till tomorrow." Bobby closed his eyes and pretended he didn't understand the jab.

Following Danielle to the emergency room, Gloria passed her own house and saw Kristen's red minivan parked in the driveway. She sighed in relief. She could shut off one mental alarm, anyway.

They walked Bobby into the emergency room lobby, his socked feet sliding on the tile floor. He was nearly gray. Frail though he was, Gloria found his weight heavy across her shoulders.

The nurse on duty rushed to help, and Gloria surrendered her place. As the nurse, Danielle, and Bobby walked through the silver double doors,

Gloria halted. She'd stepped through hospital doors too many times in her life. No need to rush into things today.

She took a seat in the lobby, where orange plastic chairs were bolted in place facing a TV. Gloria dutifully watched a young man duct-tape one hundred and forty-four bottle rockets to each shoe. He was preparing to light them and jump over a swimming pool. Gloria assumed that the show was the video version of a Southern boy's last words: "Hey, y'all, watch this!"

He had just taken a flaming plunge into the water when Danielle came through the double doors, irate.

"Uncle Bobby's blood pressure's going down. They want to send him on home."

"That's a bad idea." Gloria heard the edge in her own voice, and spoke more carefully. "Tell them he probably hasn't had anything to drink for hours."

Danielle cranked up her bulldozer and rolled back into the triage area.

Gloria resettled into the plastic chair. For the first time, she noticed a middle-aged man sitting nervously at the end of the row. He was wearing a garish green shirt. As Gloria gazed at him, trying to decide if she knew him, the double doors opened and an older man came through.

Gloria straightened. She did know this man.

He walked up to the man in the garish shirt. "Well, he don't think Chase got a snakebite."

"But it was all swolled up like a balloon," protested Garish. "What else could it be?"

"Don't know, but they got him all settled in. You can . . ." Garish was already walking toward the double doors.

The older man turned and caught sight of Gloria. "Well, hey there. Somebody of yours here?"

"Well, hi there." She no longer felt awkward around Virge McIntyre, but she was never quite comfortable either. "It's my brother Bobby. Why are you here?"

"My grandson Chase got bit by something at the family reunion today. What's wrong with Bobby?"

"We're not sure. He was just laying on the porch."

"Don't sound right," Virge agreed.

He was still handsome in his late sixties, with a personality to match. Gloria remembered those heady few months with him, flirting like . . . well, high school was much too long ago . . . at least like a couple of thirty-year-olds. Now, five years later, Virge's smile gave no indication that he recalled any of it.

He was, after all, married to Marilyn now.

He took out his phone. "I need to step out and call Marilyn. Left her there with that whole crazy family."

Gloria matched his friendly tone. "Hers or yours?"

"Oh, they're all hers. I gave her all my relatives when we got married." With a grin, Virge walked out of the waiting room, his phone to his ear.

He did remember. That evening on his front porch, watching the sun set over his pond, Gloria had told him that she wasn't going to marry again. "We've got kids and grandkids. You'd have to marry my family, and I'd have to marry yours. I'm too tired for that."

"Well," Virge said, "I don't want to keep on with. . . what is this? We're too old to date."

"I don't know what to call it."

Whatever it was, it was over. A year later, Marilyn confided that she expected to marry Virge McIntyre. That summer, Gloria helped plan Marilyn's wedding shower. She never stopped to figure out how much of her discomfort around Virge was regret, and how much was relief.

"Marilyn's cake!" Gloria exclaimed. She reached for her phone to call Kristen. At that moment, Danielle reappeared in the lobby.

"Okay, I told them he needs an IV. I talked to four different people, chased down one little Candy Striper and I think I made her cry. They're not listening to me. I need a good military presence for this. I called Andy."

She spoke of her husband, Gloria's son, as if he were a stone-faced Marine. Andy was actually the younger generation's superhero uncle. He was chief of the local volunteer fire department, could perform magic tricks, and knew the answer to any question that any kid came up with. He was, in short, the next Uncle Bobby.

But he had served time in the army and could do his own bulldozing when needed. Not much withstood the united onslaught of Danielle and Andy.

He arrived twenty minutes later. "Hey, Mom," he said. "Let's go find a doctor."

Gloria trailed her son—tall and dark-haired like Jim—through the double doors. The white-tiled hallway stretched in front of her, and the air was filled with the sterile-sweet smell of anxiety and loss.

Andy strode ahead, but Gloria paused at the curtain where Virge's grandson, Chase, lay with his leg swathed in bandages. Sitting at his bedside was Garish (now that she knew he was Virge's son, Gloria recalled that his name was Dennis and he lived somewhere out West). Chase was saying, "Well, I did notice that spot on my leg yesterday."

Andy had cornered a harried-looking doctor whose nametag said *Ashley Bentley*. It unnerved Gloria that today's professionals had names that she still associated with middle-schoolers.

Dr. Bentley said tiredly, "There doesn't seem to be any need to keep him here. I already told your wife that. So did the nurses. All of us. Repeatedly."

"You've got to keep him here, or you've lost him," Andy answered. "He won't come back."

Gloria chimed in. "Once Bobby gets back home, he'll dig in one and a half heels and refuse to budge."

"He'll be dead in two days."

"Or sooner. I doubt he's had anything to drink all day."

"All right." Dr. Bentley held up her hand briefly. "We can keep him for an IV." Her cell phone buzzed, and she answered it with alacrity. Gloria suspected she'd have welcomed a bus wreck if it meant she could escape Bobby's family.

Andy went to find Danielle, and Gloria pulled aside the pale blue curtain to Bobby's room. He opened his eyes when he heard her. Bobby never shouted and raged; instead, he fumed like a volcano oozing lava. "I guess they're going to make me stay. Damn meddling family."

"You're welcome."

"I'm going to lose my turnips."

"At the rate you're going, we'll be able to bury you with them."

Bobby glared at the wall in silence.

A nurse arrived with an IV. Danielle and Andy crowded into the tiny room behind Gloria. Dr. Bentley pushed her way to the bedside and examined Bobby quickly and efficiently. "Blood pressure's much better, no sign of a virus. It could be an infection."

"I think he would have noticed if something got that infected," Danielle argued.

Bobby cleared his throat. "Well," he said. "Could be that sore on my foot. Been there for a while."

Gloria, Danielle, and Andy stared at him. Dr. Bentley said, "Let me see it."

Slowly Bobby worked the sock off his right foot. His jaw was clenched against the pain. As the sock slid free, he lay back, wiping sweat off his forehead with a trembling hand.

Dr. Bentley frowned at the foot. "That's some sore. Could be a spider bite. Second one I've seen today—they're bad this summer."

"Uncle Bobby! You knew about that and didn't tell us?" Andy exclaimed.

"How long is 'a while'?" Danielle chimed in.

Bobby glared at the wall.

"Well, I guess you are staying, then," said the doctor. "We'll call the surgeon who did the operation on your foot." Rubbing her temples, Dr. Bentley shouldered through the smoldering family ties and hurried away.

"Bobby!" Gloria said. "Why'd you let this go so long?"

"My turnips," Bobby growled. "Two rows of them. Gary Bledsoe said he'd buy them. Says mine are the best he can get."

Gary Bledsoe ran the farmer's market in town and paid Bobby well for his produce. Suddenly Gloria understood.

"We'll take care of the turnips," she said.

"You should have asked us to do it!" Andy said. Bobby just closed his eyes again, weary but relieved.

Outside the room, rapid footsteps sounded. Kristen's brown curly head appeared around the curtain. "Mom!" she whispered loudly. "I just found out. How is he?"

"Sick," Gloria said distractedly. "How'd the cake turn out?"

"What cake?"

"Didn't you get my text?"

Kristen pulled out her phone. "Oh. I didn't see it. Marilyn told me about Uncle Bobby so I came right over."

It was odd that Kristen said "Marilyn" instead of "Melissa," but a more urgent thought filled Gloria's head.

The cake.

Gloria clutched her purse. "Darn it! I've got to go. I might be burning down my house right now! All for a darn cake for a darn surprise party for a darn friend!"

Only Gloria didn't say *darn*. Although ladies of Gloria's generation did not swear, Jim had encouraged a cuss or two for certain situations. Even he would be impressed now.

She drove home with her hazards on, both hands on the wheel, muttering imprecations upon Bobby, spiders, and chocolate cakes. She watched anxiously for any sign of smoke as she rounded the last curve to her home.

The white house with its gray shutters and the two old magnolias framing it appeared unharmed. Gloria struggled out of the driver's seat. Days like this definitely made her feel her age, whatever that was. She scuttled up the porch steps and held her breath, preparing to enter a smoke-filled house.

She was greeted by the warm scent of chocolate cake.

Hurrying to the kitchen, Gloria stared in amazement. The cake was not just baked. It was frosted with three hues of blue, swirling together in a crashing wave at the foot of a white-sand beach made of sugar and crushed cookies. Two plastic rainbow-colored umbrellas cast shade over a tiny cooler with teeny margarita glasses and a pair of flip-flops.

"You like it?" asked a voice behind her.

Gloria turned to see Marilyn on the living-room couch. "Did you do this?"

"Sure did. The decorations were there on the counter."

"What are you even doing here?"

Marilyn smiled. "Virge told me Bobby was in the ER, so I was going to come see you at the hospital. Kristen was here, so I stopped to ask her about it. Turns out she hadn't even heard yet."

"But the cake . . ."

"Smelled it through the window. I knew you weren't going to want to fuss over a cake after being at the ER."

Gloria glanced at the clock. It had been over two hours since she got Danielle's phone call. "Well, thank you! It's beautiful."

"It wouldn't make *House&Home*, but I thought the beach decorations looked real inviting. Wish I could go for my birthday. It's tomorrow, you know."

"Oh, is it?" Gloria said, limping to her recliner.

"I don't expect everybody to remember." But Marilyn sounded a little wistful. "So how's Bobby?"

"I think he'll be okay. We got to the hospital in time."

"Oh, good. I'm waiting for Virge to call back with news about his grandson Chase . . ."

"Spider bite," Gloria said.

It was Marilyn's turn to be surprised. "You sure?"

"Seems they're pretty bad this summer."

"Well, thanks. We were pretty worried." Marilyn smiled faintly. "I guess you got hospital duty for two families today."

Slumped in her recliner, her weary legs stretched out in front of her, Gloria laughed. She couldn't stop; she laughed until she was out of breath.

On the wall across from her, Jim smiled.

The end

A Note...

Thank you for reading! As an indie author, I rely on readers to spread the word about my books. If you enjoyed these stories, please consider leaving me a review and telling others about this collection.

Also, check out my novel, *The Fellowship*.

I blog at SaraRobertsJones.com. Be sure to let me know you dropped in!

About the Author

Sara Roberts Jones is a Mississippi girl who married a Canadian boy, so they compromise and live in Virginia with their four children.

This page intentionally left blank.

For spy notes.

Or a grocery list.

Whichever you happen to need first.